# The Maya

sacred symbols

# The Maya

Thames and Hudson

# THE MAYA

The Spanish Conquest was foreseen by the Maya prophet Chilam Balam: 'Receive your guests, the bearded men, the men of the east, the bearers of the sign of God...'.

*Opposite* Map of the lands occupied by the Maya, showing the principal sites.

**Frontispiece** Mayan courtly ritual: musicians portrayed in a mural at Bonampak, A.D. 790.

Modern commentaries term the area in which the Ancient Maya lived as Mesoamerica, characterized both as a geographical region and as a cultural entity. Its peoples shared the 260-day calendar, various elements of religious practice and belief, including blood-letting and human sacrifice, and a sense of common culture, manifested in agriculture, architecture and even game-playing. The principal lands of the Maya – a society driven by ritual and symbolism – lay in present-day Yucatán, Guatemala and Honduras.

Isla Cerritos

Komchen
Dzibilchaltun
Izamal
Oxkintok
Mayapan
Chichen Itza
Coba

Uxmal
Kabah
Sayil
Labna
Tulum

Island of Cozumel

NORTHERN
LOWLANDS

Edzna

CAMPECHE

QUINTANA ROO

GULF OF MEXICO

Xicalango

Becan
Rio Bec
Nohmul
Cerros
Calakmul
Cuello

CARIBBEAN SEA

TABASCO

El Mirador
Rio Azul
Lamanai
Nakbe
San Jose

Palenque

Uaxactun
Holmul

Piedras Negras
Tikal

Barton Ramie

Yaxchilan

SOUTHERN
LOWLANDS

CHIAPAS

Bonampak

Altar de Sacrificios
Seibal
Dos Pilas

NORTHERN HIGHLANDS

Lake
Izabal

Quirigua
Naco

Izapa

Copan

SOUTHERN HIGHLANDS

PACIFIC OCEAN

Kaminaljuyu

Mexico
Guatemala
Belize
El Salvador
Honduras

# cities and sites

Unlike other cultures in Mesoamerica, the Maya flourished in a multiplicity of centres. One substantial reason for this was the ability of the various communities to communicate through an ever more sophisticated language of great symbolic richness. By the Classic period competing city states had emerged all over the Maya lands: Caracol, Copán, Piedras Negras, Tikal, Bonampak and, eventually, the great centre of Palenque. In the 9th century A.D., however, the wealth and power of the Maya seem to have suffered rapid collapse, leaving only separate regional centres to flourish until the Spanish Conquest. By this time the Mayan cities often had several layers of buildings and remains.

Tikal, Guatemala, from the air.

The city of Tikal
covered six square
miles and comprised
about 3,000
structures, ranging
from temples to huts;
estimates of the total
population vary
between 10,000 and
40,000.

# time and the maya

**t**he history of the Maya is divided into three periods: the Preclassic, from 1500 B.C. until A.D. 200; the Classic, A.D. 200–900; and the Postclassic, from A.D. 900 to the Spanish Conquest. The Maya reckoned time by two calendars: Long Count or Calendar Round. Long Count dates were derived from a 360-day year, known as a tun, divided into 18 months of 20 days. The Calendar Round had two versions: the Haab of 365 days, and the Tzolkin of 260 days.

A schematic representation of the Maya calendar.

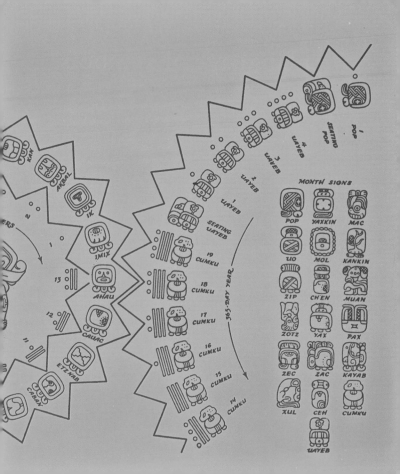

KAN

AKBAL

IK

IMIX

AHAU

CAUAC

ETZNAB

CABAN

2

1

13

12

11

SEATING
POP

1
POP

4
UAYEB

3
UAYEB

2
UAYEB

1
UAYEB

SEATING
UAYEB

19
CUMKU

18
CUMKU

17
CUMKU

16
CUMKU

15
CUMKU

14
CUMKU

365-DAY YEAR

MONTH SIGNS

POP   YAXKIN   MAC

UO   MOL   KANKIN

ZIP   CHEN   MUAN

ZOTZ   YAX   PAX

ZEC   ZAC   KAYAB

XUL   CEH   CUMKU

UAYEB

# a language of symbols

*Symbol and metaphor pervaded the whole of the Mayan way of life and the methods of recording it. All levels of the universe, from natural objects and animals to the supernatural, carried a great weight of association and significance. The carvings on stelae, one of our primary sources of information about the Maya, reveal a world of multi-layered meaning. A house, a maize field, a great caiman or even a tortoise could represent the earth. The hieroglyphic writing of the Maya, itself a complex series of symbols, refers consistently to a world of ritual: bloodletting, accession, birth, burial and kingship.*

**Approximately 85 per cent of Classic Mayan inscriptions can now be read, making the civilization the only historical one in the New World with comprehensive records, stretching back to the 3rd century A.D.**

*Opposite* A leaf from the Dresden Codex, reproduced in Humboldt's atlas of 'Nouvelle Espagne', Paris, 1810.

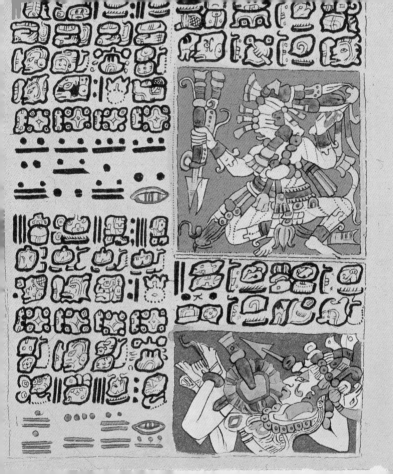

# THE SACRED COSMOS

To the Maya the universe was wholly alive with spiritual power and symbolism: all natural phenomena, supernatural beings and humans played linking parts in one great cosmic ritual. The overall context for this action was viewed as a three-part structure: the Overworld, the Middleworld, and the Underworld. The first was probably viewed as the day sky, illuminated by the sun, but the night sky was identified with the Underworld which therefore was seen to pass over humanity daily. This was of especial significance to the Maya who regarded the movement of heavenly bodies as indicative of the actions of the gods. The Middleworld was that of humans, with the four cardinal points of the compass designated by a tree, a bird, and a colour.

The Mayan cosmos, a complex structure of symbolism and ritual,
shown on a Late Classic polychromed tripod plate, c. A.D. 600–800.

# the sacred tree

*the three levels of the Mayan universe were joined by a central tree, an* axis mundi, *its roots plunging into the Underworld and its branches reaching to the Overworld, the heavens. This central tree was associated with the colour green, while four further trees in the Middleworld, signifying the cardinal directions, were designated by red, white, black and yellow. The red tree signified the East and the rising sun; the white, the North and the ancestral dead; the yellow, the South, right hand of the sun; the black, the West and the Underworld.*

**By the Late Classic period the Mayan sculptors had begun to excel at low relief carving, displaying a new dynamism in figure work.**

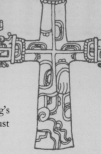

The Tree of Life is shown growing from the king's body on the sarcophagus lid of Pacal (*d.* 31 August A.D. 683) (*opposite*), Temple of Inscriptions, Palenque, Mexico.

# creation

*Befitting a people obsessed with calendars and time, the Maya were very precise in their placing of the creation of the world, the final version of which was thought to have begun on 13 August 3114 B.C. They also believed that the world had been created and destroyed at least three times. The most important surviving sacred book of the Maya, the* Popol Vuh, *recounts that creation took place through dialogue between the gods Tepen and Gucamatz, whereby the Earth was raised up from the primordial sea. Humanity was created by the gods sprinkling their own blood on the ground bones of previous generations.*

A symbol of creation, the Maize God Hun Hunahpu rises from a turtle's back, a symbol of the Earth, circled by the Hero Twins, on a plate dating from the 8th century A.D.

# the hero twins

A number of deities and mythological figures appear as pairs or triads in Maya art and legend. The most famous of these were the Hero Twins, Hunahpu and Xbalanque, whose adventures are recounted in the Popol Vuh, the most thorough account of the creation of the Mayan people and the birth of their religion. The twins were notably expert in the Mayan ballgame; summoned by the lords of Xibalba, the gods of the Underworld, to demonstrate their prowess, the twins survive a series of tests, finally to defeat the Death Gods. The last stage of this contest sees the Twins perform a series of apparent miracles, bringing the dead back to life. The lords of the Underworld beg to be sacrificed so that they too can experience the return to life. The Twins comply, but omit the resurrection!

The meeting of the Hero Twins with the god Itzamna depicted on a yellow and orange painted vase (*opposite*), Mexico, c. 593–830.

# the earth

One common metaphor for the Earth in the Maya bestiary was the caiman, evoking the image of mountainous land floating on the original waters of creation. The varied phenomena of the Earth — mountains, rivers, earth itself, caves and sky — were all thought by the Maya to have their own intense spiritual life. Another model for the Earth was the maize field, the growing of which symbolized the creation of the Mayan world.

The Maya believed the earth to be flat with four corners at the cardinal points, to which they ascribed colours: red for east, white for north, black for west, yellow for south, and green in the centre.

A tripod bowl with lid; the handle is in the form of a spotted turtle,
a common symbol of the Earth, Guatemala, c. 495–593.

This section of a Late Classic cylinder vase shows the Three Stone Place (a deity is sitting on three stones) where the gods created the universe by separating the heavens from earth, *c.* 672–830. Skybands (*opposite*) included symbols for the various heavenly bodies.

# the heavens

**t**he skies were a deep source of mystery to the Maya, a realm of supernatural happenings with which they associated some of their most potent symbolism. The harpy eagle and the Muan Bird, a horned owl, were both symbols of the sky and of the 20-year katun period. In common with other Mesoamerican civilizations, the Maya believed the sky to be supported by gods, the Skybearers.

Throughout the year the Maya conducted rites and ceremonies to urge the heavens to provide the conditions to increase the abundance of crops and game.

# sun

The Maya had a special regard for the Sun and associated some of their most powerful gods and animal deities with it: both the jaguar and the eagle were solar creatures. A sign for the Sun first appears in the Proto-classic Maya period where it is shown as a four-petalled form known as the kin, Mayan for 'sun' or 'day'. This motif also appears on the brow of the main sun god, Kinich Ahan, of the Classic and Postclassic periods. Another sun god is the deity designated as GIII of the Palenque Triad; he represents Mayan kingship, drawing together the concepts of ruler and Sun.

The main face represented on this flanged votive cylinder (*opposite*) represents the Sun, embellished with the Earth Monster below and a fantastic headdress above, Palenque, Mexico, *c.* 690.

Eclipses were of special interest to the Maya; seven pages of tables are devoted to them in the Dresden Codex. By the middle of the 8th century A.D. they had worked out when eclipses were likely to occur.

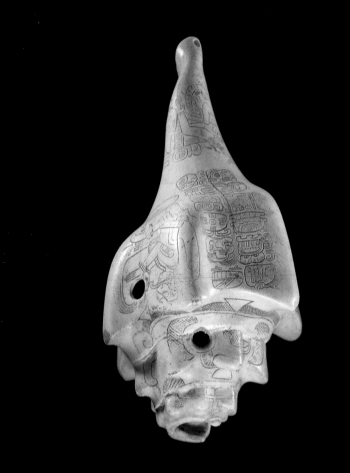

# moon

In Mayan cosmology the Sun was associated with the male principle and the Moon emphatically with the female. For the Maya of the Classic period the Moon was represented by a beautiful goddess, usually shown sitting in the crescent of the Moon, holding a rabbit. This animal, too, had a specific association with the Moon, especially when full, in that its shape can be discerned in the darker areas. A legend current among the modern Maya tells how the Moon's luminosity was diminished after a marital quarrel with her husband the Sun in which she lost an eye.

A masterpiece of Maya art: a conch shell trumpet showing the faces of three deities, including Balam-U-Xib, or 'Jaguar Moon Lord', Early Classic period, A.D. 300–500.

# venus

**The Mayan Venus had connotations of blood and war; when it appeared as the Evening Star on 29 November A.D. 735, this was taken as the sign for two rival cities to attack Seibal in the Petén.**

the amatory associations of the planet in Western cultures were very much alien to the Mayan view of this heavenly body, which always took the form of a male god. The Maya kept close astronomical watch on the two distinct phases of Venus as the Morning Star and the Evening Star, and the wars of the Maya of the Classic period were often timed to begin on the day on which Venus rose in whatever new manifestation. Both the G1 god of the Palenque Triad and Hunahpu, one of the Hero Twins, shared a twin association with the Sun and with Venus.

This leaf from the Dresden Codex (*opposite*) records the movements of the planet Venus, Humboldt's atlas of 'Nouvelle Espagne', Paris, 1810.

# DIVINE BEINGS

This rollout view of a Late Classic cylinder vase from Naranjo, Guatemala, (*opposite*) shows God L in his Underworld palace, facing six other gods of Xibalba.

Ritual and symbolism provided the bridges in the Maya world view between the worlds of humans and the gods. The deities and rites of kingship were of especial importance, since they lent supernatural authority to the ruler. The gods of the Maya take various forms, often with animal attributes – such as jaguar, serpent and eagle features – and are represented in art and architecture by both pictorial and glyphic iconography.

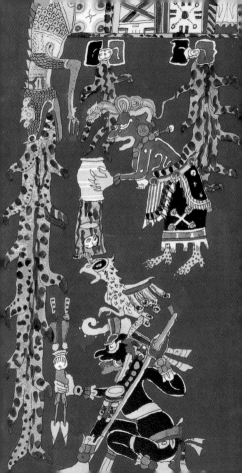

# celestial creatures

**a**lso known as the Bicephalic Monster and the Cosmic Monster, the Celestial Monster has a single body with two heads, one at each extremity, symbolizing the opposition of Venus and the Sun. This crocodilian creature often adorned, in sculptural form, the western side of buildings, a reference to Venus leading the Sun out of the Underworld – the night. The Celestial Bird (Principal Bird Deity) was probably based on the king vulture. It was seen as evil in the Popol Vuh, *in which its death heralds a new era of hope for the Maya.*

The seventy-fourth leaf of the Dresden Codex (*opposite*) shows the composite nature of the Celestial Monster: Venus, sun, sky and darkness.

The Celestial Monster in the form of altarpiece, Copán, Guatemala (*above*).

# itzamna and ancient gods

In the late nineteenth century the scholar Paul Schellhas identified a number of gods from ancient Maya screenfolds and designated each with a letter of the Latin alphabet. Of special significance were the toothless ones, who presided over Xibalba, the Underworld, Gods D, L and N. God D, with the glyphic name Itzamna ('Lizard House'), had the face of an old man, with square eyes, spiral pupils, and a disc on his brow. High god of the Maya, he was often shown as a king ruling over lesser gods; he was also closely associated with the Celestial Bird. God L, also sometimes depicted with a square eye, was characterized by the Muan Bird headdress.

God L, seated on a bench, is attended by five young women, as he watches the Hero Twins demonstrate their skill at bringing the dead back to life; painted cylinder vase, Mexico, *c.* 593–830 (*opposite*).

# pauahtun

*One of the most complex deities of the Maya pantheon, Pauahtun was a quadripartite Skybearer, appearing sometimes in a conch or shell, sometimes in*

Hunahpu, one of the Hero Twins, pulls God N from his shell before killing him; ceramic cylinder vase, Guatemala, *c.* 672–830.

*a spider's web. Always represented with
a net headdress, he was also the god of thunder
and mountains, while an ancient form of him
was associated with the monkey scribes and
therefore with writing and art. He is god N in
the Schellhas classification of the ancient deities.*

The largest human
sculpture found at
Copán is a colossal
stone head of
Pauahtun which
decorated the roof
of a massive temple.

# jaguar

**Mayan kings and nobles dressed in a variety of garments from this king of the rainforest – pelts, headdresses, even sandals and beads – to reinforce their authority.**

This vase decoration (*opposite*) shows the Water-lily Jaguar surrounded by flames as he presides over a self-decapitation.

*Central to the zoomorphic symbolism of the Maya, the jaguar was one of the most worshipped beasts of the Ancient Americas. The Jaguar God of the Underworld, hooked nose and hair knotted, was sometimes shown riding a great caiman from west to east; he was also the favourite motif on the shields of Maya warriors, probably because he was regarded as a god of war. The associations of the Baby Jaguar were equally sinister, since he is most often found with Chac, the god of rain and lightning, in scenes from the sacrificial death dance. His place in this central ritual is sometimes taken by the Water-lily Jaguar, so-called because of the water-lily blossom or leaf on his head.*

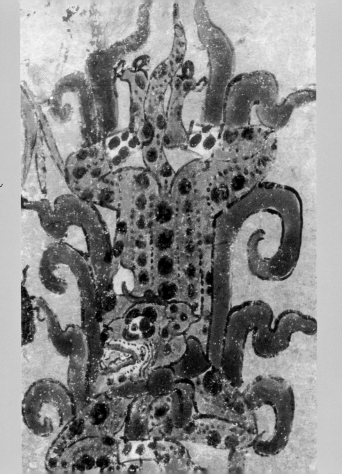

# the jester god

*this intriguingly named deity had little to do with courtly mirth; the term is derived from the resemblance of his three-pointed forehead to the cap of the medieval merrymaker. The head form was almost certainly a sign of royalty translated from the three-pointed headband which was the crown of the Mayan kingship in the Preclassic period. Later, the god sometimes took the form of a shark and often appeared as regal head ornament, made of jade. This material had a special significance among the Maya as their most precious mineral, identified with water, sky and vegetation.*

**Jade enjoyed a very special status among the Maya and was the material used for some of their finest carving. Plaques and objects were widely traded between the various Mayan lands.**

The figures of the Jester God (*opposite*) were always carved in jade or other precious green stones; until the collapse of the Classic Maya in the 9th century, this was also the form of the ruler's crown, Late Classic period, A.D. 600–800.

This figure of the young Maize God once graced a temple at Copán, Honduras, *c.* A.D. 775. His youthful looks and the foliage surrounding his head symbolize his association with the young maize.

# the maize god

the Maize God of the Early Classic period of the Maya appears as an attractive youth with maize leaves springing from the top of his head. Two later forms of the god have been identified: the Tonsured Maize God and the Foliated Maize God. The former was associated with one of the Hero Twins of Popol Vuh and is so named because areas of his head appear shaved. Recently discovered murals show the god's head as ripened ears of corn, suggesting an association with the matured maize crop. 'Foliated', however, has only one maize ear springing from his head and may therefore have stood for the crop during growth.

Maize was very much at the centre of Maya civilization, but other crops were grown. Every household had its own kitchen garden.

# the paddler gods

The main image on this splendid vase (*opposite*) – its colours painted on cream slip – shows the journey of the soul to the Underworld, rowed by the Paddler Twins in their supernatural canoe; Guatemala, *c.* 672–830.

this monstrous pair gained their name from their appearances as paddlers of the canoe of life. They are associated especially with the end of calendar periods and the blood-letting which occurred then; hieroglyphic texts give them a special relationship to the blood-letting of kings. The paddler in the bow of the canoe, *Old Jaguar Paddler*, represents night, while *Old Stingray Paddler* in the stern is the deification of day. Neither is a pretty sight: Jaguar is toothless, while Stingray has an especially aged face with a lancet, or perforator, in the septum of his nose.

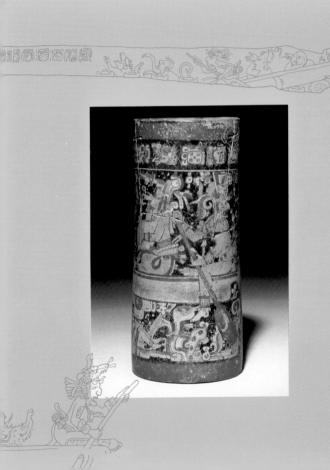

# palenque triad gods

This trio of gods only appear together in the Late Classic city of Palenque. Designated GI, GII and GIII, they were all born within three weeks of each other. Two of them were identified respectively with Chac, god of rain and lightning, and with the Jaguar God of the

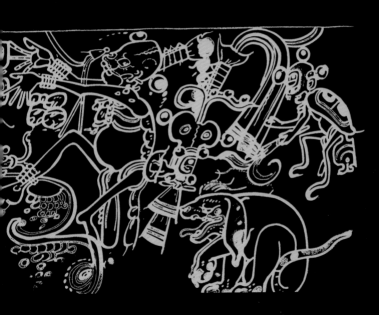

Underworld. This scene on a Late Classic cylinder vessel (A.D. 600–800) shows Chac dancing on the left, while Jaguar lies on the Cauac Monster, a zoomorphic mountain symbol. A third god, leg raised, extends his hands in frenzied dance.

# the water bird

the oldest member of the celebrated Palenque Triad, often identified as a sun god with a particularly close association with Venus, is sometimes represented as having a Water Bird headdress. This symbolic creature enjoyed pre-eminent status in the mythology and symbolism of the Maya, probably reflecting the importance of the aquatic birdlife which flourished on the canals, rivers and swamps of the Mayan lowlands. The Bird was usually shown with a fish in its beak, which resembled that of a cormorant, although its crested head was more like that of a heron.

The handle of the lid to this Early Classic tetrapod bowl (A.D. 350–500) (*opposite*) is in the form of the Water Bird. Its wings spread over the surface of the lid, while the cormorant-like head rears up to form the arch of the handle, completed by the fish in its beak.

# the monkey scribes

Patrons of writing, art and calculations,
these twins make frequent appearances
in the Maya art of the Classic period.
They are generally shown as being very
busy with the tools of their trade:
paints, books and writing brushes.
Their form was often that of the howler
monkey with a human body. They were
also identified with the twin half-
brothers of the Hero Twins
in the Popol Vuh,
Hun Batz (Howler
Monkey) and Hun
Chuen (Spider
Monkey), who had been
turned into monkeys by the
mischievous Twins.

The Monkey Scribes, both in painted and sculpted versions, were
usually represented as being extremely busy with brushes and paints,
as on this fine Late Classic vase from Copán (*above*) or as expressed
in the crouching figure (*opposite*) from the same site.

# the vision serpent

**V**arious monsters and beasts derived from local wildlife inhabit the Mayan cosmology: rearing serpents, for instance, were central to ritual, especially to penis and tongue blood-letting. Serpents are shown rearing up to spew forth gods and ancestors. They often have two quite different heads, one at either end of a smooth or feathered body, with long snouts and even beards. The association with sacrifice was frequently reinforced by making the rear head in the form of the personification of blood.

The drawing of blood from the penis took place on significant dates; the perforating instrument was a stingray spine or bone awl, usually adorned and deified.

This lintel (*opposite*) from Chiapas, Mexico (Late Classic period, *c.* A.D. 600–900), depicts the wife of a ruler holding the instruments of blood-letting. Above a second dish, presumably also a receptacle for blood, rises the Vision Serpent, symbol of contact with Gods and ancestors.

# chac, god of rain

**O**ne of the great gods of the Maya, Chac is still venerated by Mayan peoples today. His appurtenances were many and varied: catfish whiskers, reptilian snout, body scales and bound hair. He is frequently shown with an axe or serpent, indicating his status as god of lightning. His connection with water and rain is often represented by showing his image in streams of falling water, the beneficial effects of which also characterized him as a patron of agriculture and provider of maize.

This pottery incense burner from Mayapan (*opposite*) (*c.* 1200) is in the form of Chac, the Rain God. In one hand he carries a small bowl and in the other a ball of flaming incense.

# BLOOD AND KINGSHIP

The Maya practised hereditary kingship, the succession generally passing from father to son. There is, however, evidence that two of the rulers of Palenque were women. The accession to kingship was intimately

Son of Lord Pacal, the renowned ruler of Palenque, Kan-Xul accedes to the throne, his parents seated beside him; this detail (*below*) is taken from the Palace Tablet.

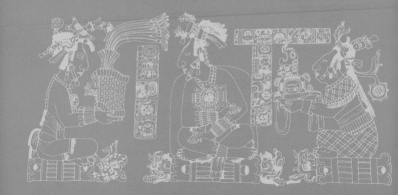

connected with blood-letting and sacrifice – the release of the substance which bound Maya society together, placated the gods and set the seal of sacred authority on the new ruler. Some surviving monuments show Mayan lords seated high above prisoners prepared for sacrifice, while bloody footprints marked the steps of the king to his throne. And, in Classic Maya art, the king himself is often represented in the act of sprinkling blood, recalling the creation.

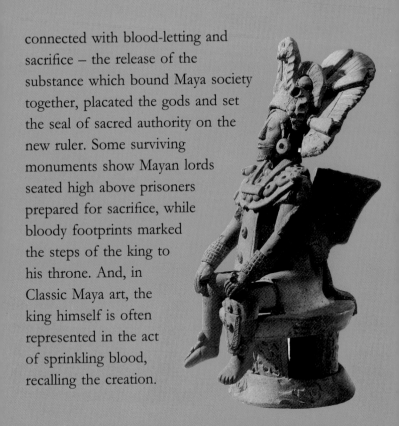

# strife and warfare

**W**ar, *with its attendant possibilities of capture and subsequent sacrifice, provided a rich vein of symbolism for the Maya, and monuments celebrating battles are numerous. Hereditary kingship was the customary political system of the Mayan city-states and, in spite of family ties, it was a structure which often led to armed confrontation. The captives from the vanquished side provided a ready supply of sacrificial victims for the blood rituals so necessary for the stability of Maya society. Warfare in the Late Classic period became more a means of territorial expansion than of support for a world of symbol and ritual.*

The costumes worn by the figures on this Late Classic carved lintel from Piedras Negras (A.D. 667) designate them as lords (standing) and warriors (kneeling). Capes made of broad strips were worn by both groups.

# lord pacal

**U**nique among all Mesoamerican pyramids, the Temple of the Inscriptions at Palenque was almost certainly built as a funerary monument on the orders of Pacal, one of the greatest of the city-state rulers. Pacal became king at the age of twelve and ruled until his death at eighty in A.D. 683. A series of symbols decorate the tomb and a splendid jade mosaic mask was buried with the body. The name Pacal meant literally 'hand-shield' and could be written either as a picture of a shield or spelt out phonetically.

The funerary crypt of Pacal at Palenque was finally opened in 1952; the entrance had been deliberately concealed. Inside, a great rectangular stone slab decorated with relief carvings overlaid the actual sarcophagus.

The life-sized jade and mosaic mask of Lord Pacal (*opposite*) was found in the funerary crypt of the Temple of Inscriptions at Palenque. It was buried with the king on his death in A.D. 683.

# palenque

**U**nder Pacal, the city of Palenque became one of the most splendid in the whole of the Maya lands. For a period of about 150 years from A.D. 600 it expanded rapidly, with a massive building programme. The great palace probably took over a hundred years to build and was clearly intended to bring a new luxury to courtly life there; great stone carvings celebrated the achievements of the rulers. The carvers of Palenque used a fine limestone to make their panels; in one, Pacal's second son, who became king in A.D. 702, is shown seated between his dead parents who offer him a jade-plated headdress and shield.

The great palace of Palenque (*opposite*) yielded such treasures as this stucco head.

# the court

**O**nce a king had taken his place on the throne it was likely that he would remain in office until his death, so that he would — unless captured — be able to enjoy a lengthy court life, with all its attendant symbolism and ritual. Apart from the dimensions of sacrifice and blood-letting, there was a lighter side to life. Clowns, for instance, would have given performances in which they personified gods and demons. Court ritual also included the performance of music by singers and instrumental players equipped with an assortment of flutes, rattles, drums, gongs and conch shells.

This ceramic expression of the art of courtly love (*left*) dates from the Late Classic period. Women were quite frequently represented in Maya art, usually as one of two archetypes: the courtly woman and the courtesan — the latter appearing with Underworld deities or even rabbits.

Court life undoubtedly had a gentler, more peaceful side; this
drinking scene depicted on a Late Classic vase shows a Maya dignitary
admiring himself in a mirror held by a dwarf.

# costume

dress among the Maya was an elaborate extension of social code and symbolism. One important feature of all accession ceremonies would have been the ordering of new robes for the dignitaries in attendance. Warriors sometimes adopted costumes made from the pelts or feathers of potent animals or birds. Some Early Classic period representations show the use of coyote fur, while eagle and jaguar warriors parade at the Tula and Chichén Itzá sites. Noble women might have worn a cape and skirt with a spondylus shell waist ornament, symbolizing the womb and the Maize God, who had special significance in Maya costume.

These murals at Bonampak (c. A.D. 790) (left) depict a high-ranking dignity in glorious apparel, contrasting with the simple garments of the attendants.

# temples and tombs

the concepts of 'temple' and 'tomb' tended to overlap in the Mayan world view. The former was often constructed, as in Pacal's Palenque, to enshrine the latter. Buildings which may very well have been closer to palaces have also attracted the term 'temple' in the past. The Mayan temple proper consisted of a platform with chambers above, with access by a single staircase, also symbolizing the descent to the Underworld. In the case of the Temple of Inscriptions at Palenque a secret staircase led down to Pacal's tomb and sarcophagus, probably the most extraordinary in the whole of Mesoamerica.

One of the wonders of Mayan civilization, the seventh-century Temple of Inscriptions (*right*) at Palenque was the burial site of Lord Pacal.

# captives and sacrifice

human sacrifice was a powerful, complex symbol of the binding together of men and gods in Mesoamerican societies; it was one element in social practice which truly shocked the invading Spaniards. From the evidence of Late Classic depiction the Maya generally decapitated their victims, often after torture. The sacrifices may have been slaves bought for the purpose or captured enemies; there is some evidence that parents even sold children for the purpose. High-ranking members of an enemy were particularly prized as sacrifices, since their prestige made them a more valuable offering to the gods.

Its scalp hanging from its head, body contorted in pain, mouth open in one last, dreadful scream, this Late Classic figurine (*opposite*) of a sacrificial captive encapsulates the bloody side of life.

# blood and hearts

**a**ll Mesoamerican peoples placed a special value on blood and hearts as sacrificial offerings. The blood was a symbol of man's debt to the gods who had created him; the heart, as the most vital organ, was the most precious food for the lords of creation. Much Mayan sacrifice was by decapitation, but there is evidence that especially important occasions were symbolized by the removal of the heart.

The *Popol Vuh* refers to killer bats in the Underworld – a motif used to decorate the buildings in Maya cities in which captives were tortured and killed.

Heart offering (*opposite*) and ritual killing (*above*) were the means by which the Maya placated the gods and ensured continuing order in the cosmos.

This ballcourt marker was one of three at Copán, Honduras,
which boasts one of the most perfectly preserved of Maya courts;
it portrays the players gathered around the large rubber ball.

# the ballgame

The ritual exchange of the ballgame so fascinated the conquering Spaniards that a troupe of players was taken to Europe in 1528. The game was played between teams of two to three players; points were scored by aiming the rubber ball towards small stone rings or markers along the sides and ends of the court. Only the thighs and upper arms could be used to control it. The game probably symbolized the movement of the Sun, Moon and Venus, with the ball being seen as the Sun moving in and out of the Underworld, symbolized by the ballcourt.

The ballcourt at Copán is the most perfectly preserved of the Classic Maya period. It is built of stucco-faced masonry, with three stone markers on either side and three more set into the floor of the court.

**Overleaf** A rollout view of a panoramic depiction of the ballgame on a vase. The glyphic texts shown between the players represent the comments of the participants.

# the underworld

the best account of the ballgame and its links to the afterlife and the Underworld occurs in the Popol Vuh, where the Hero Twins, the greatest ballplayers in the world, outwit the lords of Xibalba, literally the 'place of fright' – this defeat of the old gods of death was something every Mayan had to do to achieve regeneration and rise to the heavens. But first, immediately after death, came the journey through a vile, decayed Underworld – a journey so harrowing that the deceased was buried with all manner of protective objects.

The Princeton Vase (Guatemala, c. 672–830) (*opposite*) shows the

## Sources of Illustrations

The following abbreviations have been used:
*a* above, *b* below, *l* left, *r* right.
The Baltimore Museum of Art. Gift of Alan
Wurtzburger: 70. Drawing by C P Beetz, after
originals by J A Fox: 61. Museum of Fine Arts,
Boston. Gift of Landon T Clay: 1, 19, 34.
Copyright British Museum: 42, 53. Drawing by
Michael Coe: 27*l*, 28, 46–7. From T Patrick Culbert
*Maya Civilization* 1993, St Remy Press and
Smithsonian Institution: 5. Dallas Museum of Art,
The Eugene and Margaret McDermott Fund in
honor of Mrs Alex Spence: 78. Copyright © 1985
Founders Society Detroit Institute of Arts,
Founders Society purchase, Katherine Margaret
Kay Bequest Fund and New Endowment Fund:
64*l*. Duke University Museum of Art, Durham,
North Carolina. Museum Purchase: 36*b*–7. From
a copy by Felipe Dávalos. Courtesy of the Florida
State Museum, Gainesville: 2. J G Fuller/The
Hutchison Library, UK: 62. Museo Popol Vuh,
Universidad Francisco Marroquín, Guatemala City:
45. From F H A von Humboldt *Nouvelle Espagne
Atlas* 1810: 11, 29. Photo © Justin Kerr: 1, 13, 17,
19, 21, 22, 26, 34, 36*b*–7, 39, 40, 45, 49, 50, 65,
70, 76–7, 79. From Viscount Edward
Kingsborough *Antiquities of Mexico* Volume III
1830: 32. Finn Lewis/The Hutchison Library, UK:
7. From A P Maudslay *Biologia Centrali Americana*
Volume II 1889–1902: 52. Instituto de Cultura de
Tabasco, Dirección de Patrimonio Cultural, Museo
Regional de Antropologia "Carlos Pellicer Cámara",
Villahermosa, Mexico: 24. Museo Nacional
Antropologia, Mexico: 55, 57. Drawing by Mary
Miller: 64*r*. New Orleans Museum of Art. Ella
West Freeman Foundation Matching Fund: 49,
Women's Volunteer Committee Fund: 51.
American Museum of Natural History, New York:
63. J Pate/The Hutchison Library, UK: 69.
Courtesy Peabody Museum, Harvard University,
Cambridge: 59, 66, 73. Edwin Pearlman, M.D.,
Norfolk, Virginia: 26. Drawing by Diane Griffiths
Peck: 31. The Art Museum, Princeton University.

Gift of the Hans and Dorothy Widenmann
Foundation: 79. Private collection: 13, 21, 22.
Copyright Merle Greene Robertson, 1976: 14, 60.
The Saint Louis Art Museum. Gift of Morton D
May: 76–7. Drawing by Linda Schele: 15, 23, 27*t*,
33, 36*a*, 44, 45, 48, 56, 72*r*. From Paul Schellhas
*Representation of Deities of Mayan Manuscripts* 1904: 54.
From Robert J Sharer *The Ancient Maya* 1994 5th
edition, Stanford University Press, Stanford,
California: 38. Drawing by Karl Taube: 8, 16, 18,
20, 41, 71. Antonio Tejeda: 66. After J E S
Thompson *The Rise and Fall of Maya Civilization*
1956, University of Oklahoma Press: 9. From
Wilson G Turner *Maya Designs* 1980, Dover
Publications, Inc. New York: 74. Utah Museum of
Fine Arts, Salt Lake City. Permanent Collection: 40.

*First published in the United States of America in 1996
by Thames and Hudson Inc., 500 Fifth Avenue,
New York, New York 10110*

*Library of Congress Catalog Card Number 95-61825*
ISBN 0-500-06022-3

*Printed and bound in Slovenia*